S is for Sea Glass

A Beach Alphabet

Written by Richard Michelson and Illustrated by Doris Ettlinger

A is for Angel

When we're at the seashore the first thing I've planned
Is to lie really flat with my back in the sand.

I'll hold my arms close, then I'll stretch them out wide,
Sliding up overhead and back down to my side.

I'll sweep my legs outward, then swing them back straight,
Like I'm opening and closing a fairy-tale gate.

And when I stand up, Mom will say that she sees
The sand robes and wings of the angel in me.

B is for Boardwalk

I'm walking with Dad down the boardwalk.
Look. A mime!
And a girl on guitar.
We stop at the Snack Shack for Black Jacks
And a T-shirt that says where we are.
This sign points toward ice cream.
That line's for the potty.
The sun is beginning to set.
We've walked down the boardwalk
each day of this week but…
we haven't reached
the beach
yet.

Soft ICE CREAM open

SNACK SHACK open

RESTROOM

Arcade

NO BICYCLES ON BOARDWALK EXCEPT 6AM-10AM

LIFEGUARD ON DUTY

C is for Castle

I've built a grand castle with turrets and towers
    And parapets, arrow slits, keeps, and a moat.
I've battled the seagulls and land crabs for hours;
    The coastline is littered with seaweed I smote.

Even the big kids have come to pay tribute;
    My name is known far and my fame has spread wide.
But the end is at hand for my kingdom of sand—
    Alas, nothing can save us from waves at high tide.

Off my leash   running up the beach
Wet sand in my fur   sniff the salt air
Chase a seagull   stop, pee, smell
A ball near the water's edge   I'll fetch it
A stick in the waves quick, I'll save it
Dive into the surf   woof woof woof
Paddle too far   back to shore
Find someone dry   shake off nearby
Off my leash   running down the beach
There's my boy   pure joy!!!

D is for Dog

E is for Empty Shells

You find us lying on the beach
And think we're just some empty shells
But we each have our stories to tell.
  We were once clams. Happy? You bet!
  Till someone showed up with a net.
If you display your shells with pride
Remember mollusks lived inside
  Before we all died—steamed or fried.

F is for Flip-Flops

Winter is buckles and shoehorns and laces
And wingtips, galoshes, and high-tops,
But summer is giggles and smiling faces
And wiggling our toes into flip-flops.

G is for Gull

You call us scavengers, unclean;
Because we eat the rinds and scraps
Left over from your fine cuisine.
Are gulls duller than you? Perhaps.

We've never called ourselves refined
And true, we have an awful screech
But gulls don't leave their trash behind—
It's not we who litter the beach.

H is for Horizon

Where does the sea stop and the sky begin?
Where does the sun rise when the dawn slips in?
Where does the ship sail when its sails disappear?
Is it under the ocean? Is it up in the air?

If I travel the world or stay here on this beach,
The horizon will always be just beyond reach.
But it's real as my dreams and it's always nearby—
That magical line where the sea meets the sky.

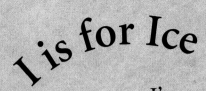

I is for Ice

I've never been here in the winter before.

Waves, like waiters, keep bringing ice cubes to the shore

Which looks like a magical ice castle floor

Of diamonds that shimmer and crystals that glisten,

And when the wind blows I can hear if I listen

The King who keeps roaring for more ice, and more.

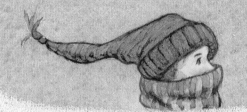

J is for Jellyfish

My colors are iridescent

Like jewels befit for a king.

If the light hits just right I will sparkle

Like a diamond inset on a ring.

But yell out my name and folks swim for the shore

Because Jellyfish means just one thing:

MY STING!

K is for Kite

Today we have gone fishing. Dad's excited, so am I.

He's angling in the ocean. Me? I'm fishing in the sky.

Dad cast his line. Hours have passed. He hasn't had one bite.

I feel a sharp tug on my string. Hurray, I've caught a kite.

My catch is big and colorful, and trails a bow-tied tail.

My dad is packing up his bait, his hooks, his rod and reel.

When I get home, I'll show my prize and put it on display.

When Dad gets home he'll tell tall tales of fish that got away.

L is for Lighthouse

I don't want to be president and live inside the White House.
I'd rather be the resident key keeper of this lighthouse.
Mom's happy she's a doctor and my dad, he loves to teach.
But me, when I grow up, I never want to leave the beach.

M is for Mosquito

Mom says God never makes mistakes.
    SLAP. CLAP. Stuff happens for a reason.
The sun—**SLAP**—shines, the surf—**CLAP**—breaks.
I'm happy every summer season.
    SMACK. WHACK. I wonder, even so,
Why—**THWACK**—God made the mosquito.

N is for Nautilus

We lived upon the ocean floor
Before the age of the dinosaur
Yet we've survived, we're doing fine
Due to our shell's spiral design.

O is for Ocean

O this is my ode to the ocean,
Which flows over most of the earth.
It's water that set into motion
Life's cycles of death and rebirth.

O the ocean is full of emotion.
What are waves but its hopes and its fears?
Where a crash has just been, new waves always begin
So let us give praise to the ocean.
It's deep as our dreams and saline as our tears—
Now come, dears, it's time to dive in.

P is for Pail

Yellow birds on sand
Stay still when I approach. Oh!
My shovel and pail.

Q is for Quiet

The sun as it's rising
The drift of a cloud
Spiders spinning webs
Crabs scuttling
Across the ocean floor
The swimming of fishes
The wishing of wishes
The opening of a door
The thoughts in my head

These are things I can hear
When it's quiet
As I lie here in bed.

R is for Rain

Nobody's at the beach today. 'Most everyone's complaining.
 The sky is dark. The clouds are thick. And I, the rain, am raining.

 Folks let waves splash them head to toe. Do you hear any whining?
 No!
 They think it's fun to get wet when their friend, the sun, is shining.

 I cool the breeze. And fill the seas. Who's not a rainbow lover?
 So why, when I come out to play, do they all run for cover?

This gift from the ocean
Was tossed and it tumbled
Till weathered by swell waves
It crossed the wide waters
And braved the high seas.
It once was a fruit jar
Or maybe a king's cup
Or medicine bottle
That saved a young princess.
Or perhaps a pirate
Once flung his decanter
From off of the gangplank
And ninety years later
It washed up here beachside
And sparkled like jewelry—
A gift just for me.

S is for Sea Glass

T is for Tide

Each day the tide's high and each day the tide's low.
The world's full of mysteries we'll never know.

The moon orbits Earth and the tides are affected.
No matter its form, all matter's connected.

As sure as it ebbs, the tide also rises.
And each day the world is full of surprises.

U is for Umbrella

Come visit my umbrella garden
     It blooms every day in the sun.
Among many multistriped parasols
     I've planted some polka-dot fun.

     The soil is best dry and sandy
     With just a slight tropical breeze.
When conditions are right, my garden grows bright
     With colorful shady beach trees.

Mom says we need some relaxation.
Time for a family vacation.

Into the car	drive too far
Unpack	search for a snack
Find a friend	dead end
No TV	sightsee
Dog fed?	late to bed
Wake too early	Dad surly
Neighbors loud	big beach crowd
Insect bites	see more sights

We had a family vacation.
Now Mom needs some relaxation.

V is for Vacation

W is for Wave

Away from the wind, water always behaves.

But when they play together, they're mischievous knaves.

They crash things and smash things—

They tumble and rumble—

They storm and they love to make waves.

X is for X Marks the Spot

What to do?
Nothing is planned.
But here's a stick
And plenty of sand.

I'll be X,
You can be O.
I challenge you
To tic-tac-toe.

Y is for Year-Rounders

It's exciting when the crowds come
And our sleepy town awakes.

All the roads are full of sightseers
And sidewalks fill with jugglers
And the beaches burst with tourists
Eating ice cream, having picnics—
There are parties, celebrations
And fun brand-new friends to play with
And I get to stay up late sometimes
And hang out with the big kids
But sometimes I get real tired
Though I don't tell anybody
And I like it when the crowds leave
And it's quiet near the seashore
Where I'm walking with my family
Through the town that we call home.

Z is for ZZZZZZZZs on the Beach

I'm feeling amazingly lazy—
been choosing to snooze in the sun.
Dad says we should play catch, swim, exercise,
toss Frisbees, or go for a run.

But days that are blazing and hazy,
I'd rather just catch a sea breeze.
So I think I'll just finish my pizza
And cozy back down for some zzzzzzzzzs.

For the MVCMA year-rounders and summer people

—Richard

★

In memory of Cedar Grove Beach Club

—Doris

Sleeping Bear Press
315 E. Eisenhower Parkway, Suite 200
Ann Arbor, MI 48108
www.sleepingbearpress.com

Printed and bound in the United States.

10 9 8 7 6 5 4 3 2 1

Library of Congress Cataloging-in-Publication Data

Michelson, Richard.
[Poems. Selections]
S is for Sea Glass : A Beach Alphabet / Written by Richard Michelson ;
Illustrated by Doris Ettlinger.
pages cm
Summary: "Following the alphabet and using a variety of poetry forms such as free
verse, haiku, and ode, elements of the beach and seaside life are celebrated"–
Provided by publisher.
ISBN 978-1-58536-862-4
I. Ettlinger, Doris, ill. II. Title.
PS3563.I34S57 2013
811'.54–dc23
2013024895